Starting Out on the Internet
A Learning Journey for Teachers

Second Edition

M. D. Roblyer
University of Maryland University College

Merrill
Prentice Hall

Upper Saddle River, New Jersey
Columbus, Ohio

Vice President and Publisher: Jeffery W. Johnston
Editor: Debra A. Stollenwerk
Development Editor: Kimberly J. Lundy
Editorial Assistant: Mary Morrill
Production Editor: JoEllen Gohr
Production Manager: Pamela D. Bennett
Director of Marketing: Ann Castel Davis
Marketing Manager: Krista Groshong
Marketing Services Manager: Tyra Cooper

10 9 8 7 6 5 4 3 2
ISBN 0-13-110970-7

❧
Table of Contents

Dedication

for Marilyn Comet—
educational technology luminary, great lady, great friend

Preface

Why This Book Was Written

The most enduring metaphor for the Internet is that of a highway, perhaps because it is such an appropriate comparison. Highways, like the Internet, can be paths to adventure and new knowledge, ways to get quickly to destinations already known, and courses to wander casually in search of new discoveries.

However, either the paved roads of a countryside or the electronic pathways of the World Wide Web also can be a confusing collection of perplexing signs and symbols, places to get lost and frustrated, a series of dead ends. The difference between these two experiences is understanding the basics of "travel" and the resources available to help the traveler.

Many educators are beginning to recognize how important it is to "get out on the road" and begin learning a new way for themselves and their students to see the world. This book is designed to be an easy way for them to learn some of the basics required to become a skilled "Internet traveler." An old proverb holds that a journey of a thousand miles begins with but a single step. This booklet has a series of first steps to get educators started on what could be a most enlightening journey.

What You Need to Prepare for the Trip

Before setting out on a journey, some preparation always is in order. However, you needn't learn everything at once. One of the best things about the Internet is that you don't have to be a very technical person to use it, just as you need not be an auto mechanic to drive a car! At first, teachers may want to ask someone to prepare their "vehicle" for them to get them started. Later, they can learn more technical items about Internet use so they don't have to rely as much on others.

But not even the best driver's manual can substitute for driving experience; getting out on the Internet is the best way to learn it. Before you start, though, be sure you have obtained the following **two** items.

❶ An Internet-ready computer. Any veteran traveler knows that having a well-equipped vehicle can make all the difference in the quality of a trip, and so it is with the Internet. To make your Internet travel go smoothly, make sure you have a computer:

☛ *With fast enough speed and enough Random Access Memory (RAM) to do Internet tasks:*

RAM is the memory that holds programs while they are being used.

Good: 1.6 GHz speed, 128 Megabytes (MB) RAM
Better: 1.7 GHz speed, 256 MB RAM
Best: 2.0 GHz or better speed, 512 MB or more RAM

☛ *Equipped with a fast enough connection:*

Good: A computer with a 56 thousand bits per second (bps) modem, and connected to a telephone line.

Speed at which signals are sent between computers is measured in bits per second, or bps.

Better: A computer with connection via a satellite system (e.g. DISH® Network or DirectTV®), cable modem (from a cable company), or Digital Subscriber (DSL) line (from the phone company).

Best: A computer on a network (e.g., at a school) that is connected to the Internet with a T1 line or better

☛ *Equipped with browser software:* Browsers are programs that display web pages as pictures so you can look ("browse") through them and do tasks with them. The most common web browsers are:

• *Netscape Communicator®*

• Microsoft's *Internet Explorer®*

However, companies such as America Online have their own browsers. Each of these browsers has versions for Windows PC and Macintosh computers.

In this book, we will show screen examples with *Netscape Communicator®*, although others are similar. Below is an example of the Prentice Hall web site as viewed through the *Netscape Communicator®* browser.

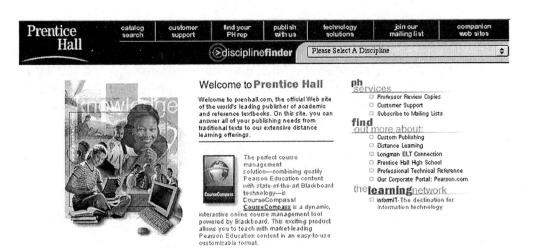

Netscape Browser Displaying the Prentice Hall Web Site

❷ **An Internet connection.** Next, you need to be connected to the Internet. What exactly does it mean to be "connected?" Although there are several different ways, they all mean you are able to use browser software to have your Internet-ready computer send electronic signals over lines and make contact with other Internet-ready computers. But access to the Internet is not free. Even schools or districts that provide it free to their teachers must pay someone for it. If you have no group that provides access for you, shop for the best **Internet Service Provider (ISP)**. Look for three things when you shop for an ISP:

Reliability: Can you get on the Internet whenever you want? Or is the line busy or is the provider's computer "down" a lot of the time?

Good support: Is someone available "24/7" (24 hours a day, seven days a week) to help you if you have problems or questions?

Fair price: Is there a reasonable flat fee, or do they charge by the minute?

If you have an Internet-ready computer and a connection to the Internet, you are ready to begin the steps in this book!

How to Use This Book

Appropriate for use either on an individual computer or in a lab setting, *Starting Out on the Internet: A Learning Journey for Teachers* takes a step-by-step approach to help you learn how to navigate the Internet and use it as a powerful resource for teaching and learning.

Look for the following icons or pictures to help guide you through each of the 11 sections:

 This "book" icon at the beginning of each section signals new Internet terms and concepts you will want to learn.

 This "light bulb" icon marks "helpful hints" or additional explanation to help you understand the new information.

 Look for this image throughout each section and at the end of each section for "Try This!" exercises for you to check your learning at each step. Answers to these exercises can be found in the Appendix of this book.

Also look for the following web site to support your learning activities:

http://www.prenhall.com/startingout

This site has two features that you can use to help develop your Internet knowledge and skills:

- **Section self-tests** – The site has a set of review questions for each section you can answer and receive immediate feedback on correctness.

- **Sample personal web site** – These web pages are used with Section 11 as you learn how to develop your own personal web site.

Enjoy the trip!

Acknowledgments

Many people look upon writing a book as an impossible undertaking. In fact, it is. But what they may not realize is how similar an enterprise it is to what classroom teachers do every day. Both involve accomplishing tasks with too little time, resources, and knowledge. Both require commitment and sacrifice: time taken away from family and friends and long hours without adequate rest or "down time." Both have teaching as their purpose and learning as their ultimate goal. But perhaps most important, both teachers and writers must love their work to make it all worth it.

My thanks go out once more to all the people who make it possible for me to do what I love. For this book, I am obliged especially to recognize my continuing debt to my friend, mentor, and editor Debbie Stollenwerk; other Merrill professionals JoEllen Gohr, Heather Fraser, Kim Lundy, Mary Morrill, and Dan Parker; my family, Bill and Paige Wiencke; and friends such as Sherry Alter and Paul Belt, Marilyn and Herb Comet, Barbara Hansen, Sharon and Jon Marshall, Mary Ann Myers, and Gwen McAlpine and Paul Zimmer.

Thanks, also, to the educators who read this book about the Internet as a way to become even better at what they do. Beginning to integrate technology into an already packed classroom and school agenda may seem impossible to others. But all we teachers know that for those who feel passionate about what they do, the difficult really is no problem, and the impossible just takes a little more time.

M. D. Roblyer
June, 2002

ONE - *Understanding URLs*
How to Use Internet Addresses

New Terms

- *Uniform Resource Locator (URL)*
- *Server*
- *Domain name*
- *Domain designator*
- *Suffix*

Required Parts of a URL

Every home in the United States has an address so people can find it and make deliveries of mail and other items. Each place you "visit" on the Internet also has an address, and for much the same reasons. However, the Internet is less tolerant of mistakes in an address than is the U. S. Post Office! Each address must be entered exactly, with every punctuation mark in place, or it will not work.

Internet addresses are called Uniform Resource Locators, or **URLs**. Look at the example URL shown below in a browser window. The line where the URL is entered is called the address line:

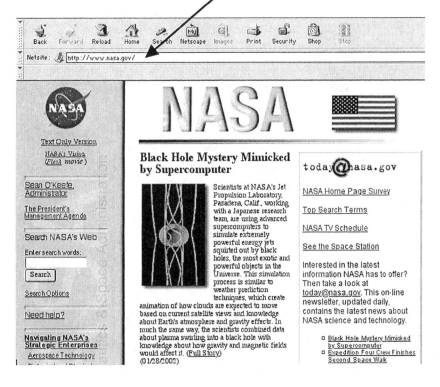

Bring up the browser on your computer screen
and enter the above URL in the address line.
Then press Return or Enter to "travel" to this address on the Internet.

Every URL has four required parts (although it can have more optional ones that will be described later):

$$\text{http://www.nasa.gov}$$
❶   ❷   ❸   ❹

❶ Each web page address begins with **http://** which stands for HyperText Transfer Protocol. The "http://" shows it is an Internet address.

❷ Most, but not all, addresses contain **www,** which stands for World Wide Web.

A "server" is a computer that has a site on the Internet.

❸ The next part of the address here is **nasa**, the name of the computer or "server" to which you connect. Every server on the Internet has an assigned label called the "domain name." **nasa** shows that this computer belongs to the National Aeronautic and Space Administration, a government agency that offers educators a wealth of resources on its web site.

Domain designators for public schools usually include the state name.

❹ Finally, another required part of the domain name, called a "domain designator," tells what kind of group owns the server. Some example domain designators are:

org = organization	**com** = business
gov = government agency	**edu** = university
k12.__.us = public schools	**net** = network
mil = military agency	**aus** = Australia

Examples: k12.ny.us (New York)

k12.fl.us (Florida)

Note that "net" is often used instead of "org" for many schools and other organizations. There are many more designators, and more are being added all the time as the need arises. The U. S. non-profit organization that sets up domain names is the Internet Corporation for Assigned Names and Numbers (ICANN).

You can learn more about ICANN at **http://www.icann.org**

Optional Parts of a URL

If an organization is a large one, it may have more than one server; or it may split up a large computer into sections. Then the domain name will have more parts. For example, the University of Maryland University College (**umuc**) has a server called **tychousa1** used for its distance courses:

http://tychousa1.umuc.edu

Optional parts called "suffixes" can come after a domain designator. Suffixes show locations on the server that are set aside for specific purposes. For example, the UMUC Academic Calendar is shown at a certain location on the UMUC server indicated by the suffix after the slash:

http://www.umuc.edu/calendar

In the spaces below, answer the following questions about the parts of the following URL.

http://www.kidlink.org/english/general/index.html

1. What does **www** stand for?

   _____

2. What is the name of the computer or server that displays this site?

   _____

3. Which part of the URL identifies this as an Internet address?

   _____

4. What is the domain designator in this URL, and what kind of group does it indicate owns this site?

   _____

5. Why are there slashes in this URL?

   _____

Three URL Uses

Three things to learn how to do with URLs are locate them, read them, and "fix" errors in them.

- **Locating URLs.** If you want to visit a site, but you don't know its URL, one way to find it is to make an educated guess. For example, let's say you want to find the website for the National Council of Social Studies. Since you know it will have an "org" designator and organizations usually use their initials in URLs, a good guess would be: **http://www.ncss.org**

Guess a URL for each of the following.
Then go on the Internet and type in the URLs to see if you are correct.

1. **National Council of Teachers of Mathematics**
   Correct answer: _____

2. **The Music Educators National Conference**
   Correct answer: _____

- **Reading URLs.** If someone gives you a URL, very often you can tell what and where it is by reading its parts. Look at an example:

http://www.noaa.gov

If you knew that the URL someone gave you was one on weather, you might guess this is for the National Oceanic and Atmospheric Administration (NOAA), a government agency that offers students and teachers a wealth of up-to-date information on the weather.

Can you read the URL for each of the following?
Type in the URL, and go to the site to see if you are right.

1. For students with vision problems: **http://www.afb.org**
   Whose site is this? _____

2. For a department in the federal government: **http://www.ed.gov**
   Whose site is this? _____

• **Fixing errors in URLs.** Someone may give you a URL with an error in it (or you may write down one incorrectly!) There are five common errors you can look for and correct:

Error #1 – Omitting one of the parts. The most common omission is the "http:// (or the "www" if it needs it).

If you have trouble with a URL, try cutting off the suffixes and going to the main page of the site.

Error #2 – Wrong domain designator. For example, people often substitute "com" for "org."

Error #3 – Punctuation errors. People often confuse forward slashes (/) and back slashes (\), and hyphens (-) with underlines (_). Also, there are no spaces in a URL. Spaces are designated with an underscore (_).

Error #4 – Punctuation omitted. If you leave out a "dot" or a slash, the URL will not work.

Error #5 – Misspellings. Most misspellings in URLs seem to occur in suffixes.

TRY THIS!

Can you spot errors in each of the following URLs?
Correct each, then enter it in a browser to check..

1. The Eisenhower National Clearinghouse, a site with lesson plans and other resources for teachers:

   What's the error? **http://enc.org** _____

2. The American School Heath Association:

   What's the error? **http://www.ashaweborg** _____

TRY THIS!

Section One
Summary Exercises: Understanding URLs

Exercises 1.1 – Review of New Terms and Concepts

_____ 1. Name for the part of the Internet address that tells what kind of group owns the server (e.g., "edu")

_____ 2. The "/roblyer" part of the following URL is an example of one of these: http://www.prenhall.com/roblyer

_____ 3. What the acronym URL stands for

_____ 4. The following URL has this kind of error: http://www.white house.gov

_____ 5. A computer that has a site on the Internet

Exercises 1.2 – Practice Activities to Expand Your Skills

1. **Locate a URL** – You try to locate the web site for the American Educational Research Association, but the URL you thought would work (http://www.aera.org) sent you to a technical association. What other URL might you try? (**HINT:** Try a different domain designator.) _____

2. **Read a URL** – Whose web site do you think each of the following is?

   http://www.ira.org/ _____
   http://peabody.vanderbilt.edu _____

3. **Fix a URL** – See if you can find and fix the errors in these URL's:

a) Apple Computer site to download their movie software:
   http://apple.edu/quicktime/download/_____

b) Organization that publishes information about educational software
   http:\\www.spa.org _____

c) A special server on the University of California at Berkeley web site with science exploration environments for K–12 schools
   http://wise.berkley.edu/ _____

TWO – *Navigating the Net*
How to Move Around in Web Pages

Five Ways to Go

You can move around from web page to web page on the Internet by using five different options. The first two options are to use two kinds of **links** that have been programmed into the web page itself. These are also known as "*hot links*" or "*hot spots.*"

These links are programmed to send your browser to another location on the Internet, either within the site or to another site, when you click on them with your mouse. These programmed links can be:

❶ Underlined text such as the ones in this NASA web page;

or

❷ Images, as in this example from the NASA web page.

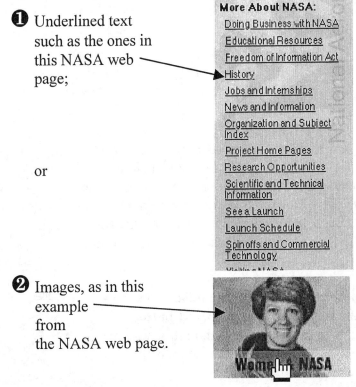

How do know when images are links? When you pass a mouse pointer over the image (without clicking) and the pointer turns into a "browser hand" such as the one on the "Women & NASA" picture above, you know it is a link. Any part of a web page can be programmed to be a link.

Three other options are available on your browser menu bars. See the NASA web page example below.

❸ **Back button**

❹ **Forward button**

❺ **Go Menu** (in *Internet Explorer*®, use **File Menu**)

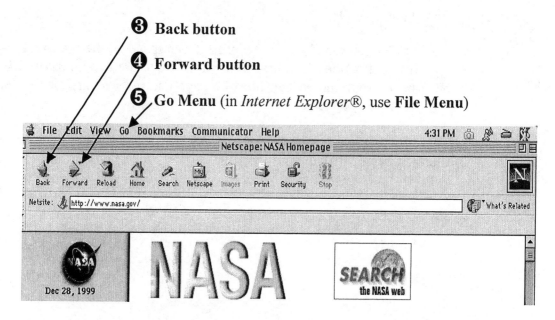

Forward and Back buttons let you go *one step at a time* on a linear path through a chain of web pages you have visited. For example, if you go to the NASA web page and click the "Educational Resources" link, you can click on the **Back button** to take you back to the NASA home page.

If you want to go back to the Educational Resources page, use the **Forward button**. You can travel back and forth in this way, just as if you were traveling back and forth visiting houses on the same road.

Notice that the **underlined links change color** after you click on them. Colors of visited and unvisited links depend on preferences specified in each browser.

More About NASA:

Doing Business with NASA
Educational Resources
Freedom of Information Act
History
Jobs and Internships
News and Information
Organization and Subject Index
Project Home Pages
Research Opportunities
Scientific and Technical Information
See a Launch
Launch Schedule
Spinoffs and Commercial Technology
Visiting NASA

*Go to the NASA home page at: **http://www.nasa.gov***
Do the following:

- Click on the "NASA for Kids" link.

- Pass your mouse pointer over the pictures on this page to locate one of the image links. Click on it.

- Click on the **Back button** twice to go back to the NASA home page.

- Click on the **Forward button** to go back though the pages you visited.

While the **Forward and Back buttons** let you go in a straight line, back and forth to pages you have been, the **Go Menu** lets you "jump around" randomly to web pages you have visited. For example:

From the NASA home page we clicked on these links:

The Go Menu is only in Netscape. In Internet Explorer, past links are listed under the File Menu.

- Educational Resources link
- Listing of Education Programs
- Educational Technology Programs

The result is the **Go Menu** listing you see here. → You can click on the **Go Menu** and scroll down to select and visit any of the pages listed there.

Go	Bookmarks	Communicator	Help
Back			⌘ [
Forward			⌘]
Home			⌘ home

✓ **Programs**
A GUIDE TO NASA EDUCATION PROGRAMS
NASA Education Programs
NASA Home Page

Create your own Go Menu listing and try it out!
*Go to a URL such as: **http://www.si.edu***
(This is the web site for the Smithsonian Institution.)
Do the following:

Click on some of the underlined and/or image links on this page. After each visit, look at the **Go Menu** and see how it has changed. Now pull down the **Go Menu** and select one of the pages listed there to travel to it.

TRY THIS!

Section Two
Summary Exercises: Navigating the Net

Exercises 2.1 – Review of New Terms and Concepts

_____ 1. Of images and text on a web page, which can be links?

_____ 2. How do you know when an item on a web page is a link?

_____ 3. What does it mean when an underlined link changes color?

_____ 4. If you want to return to a site's home page, but you had visited many of its pages since then, what would be the most efficient way to get back there?

_____ 5. What does it mean when this appears as you pass your mouse over something on a web page?   ⟶

Exercises 2.2 – Practice Activities to Expand Your Skills

1. **Navigation Aids** – Many very large, complicated web sites help site vistors by providing an at-a-glance guide called a "site map." (This will be discussed in **Section Five**.) Go to one such site: the University of Maryland University College (UMUC) web site at http://umuc.edu. What other navigation aid do you see on this page? How do you use it?

2. **More Activities with Go Menus** – Listings of pages you have visited will erase in a **Go Menu** and a new list will start when you go "down another road." For example, go the Smithsonian page, then go to other pages in this order:

    1 - The White House: **http://www.whitehouse.gov**
    2 - Library of Congress: **http://lcweb.loc.gov**
    3 - The History Channel: **http://historychannel.com**
    4 - U. S. Census Bureau: **http://www.census.gov**

All these web pages above should be listed under "Go." However, now go back to the Library of Congress and go to *another* web site, let's say, the National Weather Service (http://www.noaa.gov). Check the **Go Menu** now. The History Channel and the U.S. Census Bureau (visits 3 and 4) will not be listed now! **Go Menus** are programmed to act this way, so do not be surprised when pages you have visited are not listed anymore.

THREE – *Starting Up Search Engines*
How to Locate Information on the Internet

What Is a Search Engine?

New Terms

- *Search engine*
- *Keyword search*

Search engines are sometimes called "web crawlers."

In many ways, the Internet is a reflection of our world: a place rich in resources and information. Before the Internet, it was difficult to locate specific resources or items of information. Now there is so much information on the Internet that companies have developed special searching programs to help us locate things.

These searching programs are called *search engines*. According to Search Engine Watch, a site with information on all available search engines (http://www.searchenginewatch.com), there are many kinds of search engines. Two commonly cited types are:

❶ **Major search engine sites.** Some popular ones are:

- **All the Web**   http://www.alltheweb.com
- **Alta Vista**   http://www.altavista.com
- **Ask Jeeves**   http://www.askjeeves.com
- **Lycos**   http://www.lycos.com
- **Yahoo!**   http://www.yahoo.com

❷ **Metacrawlers.** These programs use more than one search engine at the same time to locate things:

- **Dog Pile**   http://www.dogpile.com
- **Mamma**   http://www.mamma.com/
- **Metacrawler**   http://www.metacrawler.com
- **Search.com**   http://www.search.com

Two Ways to Use a Search Engine

Both types of search engines can be used in two ways:

- **Subject index searches.** The search engine site provides a list of topics you can click on.

- **Keywords.** Type in combinations of words that could be found in the URLs of sites or documents you want.

To examine these ways, try these examples. First:

Go to the Yahoo! search engine site at:

http://www.yahoo.com

Example #1: Using subject index searches. Let's say that after reading about distance learning programs, you are wondering how many distance learning programs there are in K–12 schools. If you used "distance learning" keywords, you would get a great many higher education sites. So you might want to begin with a subject search under Education, K–12.

All the underlined text titles you see on Yahoo!'s main page actually are hot links of categories you can click on to locate Internet web sites under that heading.

The listed results of an Internet search are sometimes called "hits."

- Find and click on the link that says "Education." The search engine sends you to yet another listing.

- Find and click on the link for "K–12." It sends you to yet another listing. Click on "Distance learning," and you see a great many links related to distance programs in K–12 schools. Each link is a web page.

Example #2: Using keywords. If you know that certain words would be in the titles of web sites you are looking for, you may want to do a keyword search. Let's say you are intrigued by what you have read about voice recognition and want to locate more information. Try the following search:

- Find the box on the Yahoo! site that looks like the one below and type the words voice AND recognition (joined by the word AND).

[   ]   Search

Many sites have their own built-in search engine that lets you use keywords to search the contents of the site. Look for the phrase "Search this site."

- You also can type in whole phrases to do a search. For example, try "voice recognition" using quote marks around the phrase. Either way, you get a listing of companies and organizations that are doing things with this technology.

Search Engine Sites

Different search engines are useful for different purposes and each has its own procedures. The University of Central Florida's Instructional Technology Resource Center (ITRC) has a very useful summary of when and how to use each of the search engines. Look for it at:

http://www.itrc.ucf.edu/conferences/pres/srchtool.html

Examples taken from the ITRC site include:

- **To browse a broad topic:**
  Use Yahoo! or Lycos

- **To search for a narrow topic:**
  Alta Vista, AlltheWeb, or Google

- **To search the largest Internet amount:**
  Metacrawler or Ask Jeeves (meta-search engines)

For other types of sites (e.g., filtered ones for kids, multimedia search engines) and a wealth of information on search methods, check out Search Engine Watch at:

http://searchenginewatch.com

Keyword Search Strategies

Newer search engine sites such as Google and Ask Jeeves have natural language features built into them that make productive searches relatively easy and efficient. However, depending on the topic and the search engine you use, you may get too many hits or some may be on unintended area (e.g., Macintosh apples, rather than Macintosh computers). You can use strategies to combine keywords in ways that focus your search.

Each search engine site has its own "syntax" for joining keywords using Boolean logic operators (and, or, not). A search engine might use AND to connect the keywords:

Example: software AND evaluation

or it may allow either AND or plus signs:

Example: +software +evaluation

TRY THIS!

Try these examples on Google or Yahoo! (which uses the Google search engine software):

1. You want to see samples of computer lab rules for schools. You try the following:

"computer lab" +rules

However, you get a lot of Lab Rules for college and universities. To narrow the search and eliminate many (but not all) of the Lab Rules that aren't in K-12 schools, do the following:

"computer lab" +rules –college –university

2. Your science students want to find some sites with information on worms. When they type in "worms," they get a lot of information on worm computer viruses. So you tell them to do the following:

worm –virus

3. Your students are looking for information on the history of paper, but entering the terms "history" and "paper" yield thousands of hits on collections of papers of various historical figures. A better way would be to enter this complete phrase (quotes included):

"history of paper"

Section Three
Summary Exercises: Starting Up Search Engines

Exercises 3.1 – Review of New Terms and Concepts

_____ 1. If you wanted to locate a school's web site, and you know the name of the town where the school is located, you might select a search engine you could use in this way, rather than doing a keyword search.

_____ 2. These kinds of search engine sites use more than one search engine at once to do a search.

_____ 3. When you do a search by putting quotes around two or more words together, it makes the search look for this.

_____ 4. If you were on the web site of an educational software company to obtain information about one of its products, what search mechanism would you probably use?

_____ 5. Many search engines use this symbol for the Boolean operator "NOT."

Exercises 3.2 – Practice Activities to Expand Your Skills

Part A – Try these keyword searches:

1. Students in your literature class want more information on the Trojan Horse used by the Greeks to fool the Trojans during the Trojan Wars. When they put in "Trojan Horse," they get a lot of hits on computer viruses. What should they do to narrow the search?

2. You want to see if there are any online journals that you can use to read up on distance education. What series of terms and operators could you use?

3. KidPub (http://www.kidpub.org/kidpub) publishes children's writing and helps kids connect with other young writers. Find other web sites that support young writers.

4. Locate online French-to-English (or other languages) dictionaries. Try the same for other languages like Spanish or German.

Part B – Before doing the following searches, decide:

- *Which search engine might be best for the search?*
- *Which search method would you use: subject or keyword?*

1. **Web Sites to Support Mathematics** – Graphing calculators (or computer-based labs or CBL) are a powerful technology resource in mathematics and science content areas. Locate lesson plans that focus on graphing calculators or CBLs.

2. **Web Sites to Support History** – Locate sites that could give students information on the history of the State of Iowa (or substitute your own state).

3. **Web Sites to Support Art Education** – Locate web sites of five art museums where your students could go on "virtual field trips" to see famous paintings.

4. **Web Sites to Support Literature** – Locate a web site that has examples of Japanese haiku poetry.

5. **Web Sites to Support Writing Instruction** – Locate a web site with a rubric to judge the quality of students' written compositions.

6. **Web Sites to Support Health and Physical Education** – Locate web sites to help teach the topics of drug prevention and physical fitness.

7. **Web Sites to Support Special Education** – Many laws have been passed relating to education of students with special needs. Locate information on recent federal legislation on this topic.

8. **U. S. Department of Education Report** – Locate a report on "Computer and Internet Use Among People with Disabilities" located on the following web site: U. S. DOE website: http://ed.gov/ (**Hint:** Look for the Publications link)

9. **Technology Lesson Plans for Teachers** – Locate online lesson plans that show how to use various technologies in teaching.

10. **Technology Product Assessments** – Locate web sites with rubrics and other instruments that could help assess the quality of students' multimedia and web page products.

FOUR – *Using Bookmarks*
How to Mark Web Pages for Later Use

New Terms

How to Make a Bookmark

• *Bookmark*

You may visit so many sites on the Internet that you can quickly lose track of where you found a valuable site on a certain topic. You could write all of them down, but a quicker way is to use bookmarks.

Bookmarks is a feature in your browser. It lets you mark the address of sites you want to remember. Making a bookmark is very simple. Just travel to the site and when it is on the screen, go to the **Bookmark Menu** and select "**Add Bookmark**." A bookmark title for that site appears at the bottom of the bookmark list. See the example below for adding the Global Schoolhouse site:

In Internet Explorer®, bookmarks are listed under the Favorites Menu.

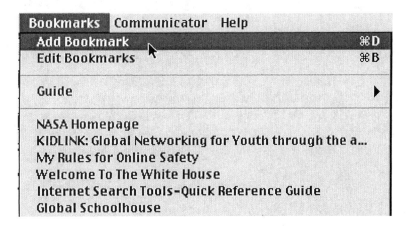

Try making a bookmark.
One site you should remember is the one for the International Society for Technology in Education (ISTE).

http://www.iste.org

Go to the ISTE site on the Internet
and create a bookmark for it.

How to Delete Bookmarks

You may want to mark some sites only temporarily, then delete them. On many browser versions, the edit feature is listed on the **Bookmark Menu** (see p. 17). Other browser versions may list it under the **Edit Menu**.

To delete a bookmark, select **Edit Bookmarks**. A window will appear with a list of your current bookmarks. Click on the bookmark you want to delete and select "Cut" or "Clear" from the Edit menu, as shown below:

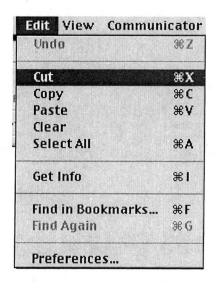

How to Organize Bookmarks

As noted in *Integrating Educational Technology into Teaching*, (Roblyer, 2003, Chapter 8) "well–prepared bookmark files are great resources for teachers and should be shared with others who have similar interests." But what is a "well–prepared bookmark file?"

For a bookmark collection to be most useful to you and others, it should be organized into sections, much like a library or any collection of materials. After you create bookmarks, you can organize them into categories of related items.

For example, let's say you are a middle school language arts teacher and you make bookmarks for the following English and Reading sites you have found:

- **International Reading Association: http://www.ira.org**

- **National Council of Teachers of English:** http://www.ncte.org

- **Teachers and Writers Collaborative:** http://www.twc.org/

- **Rensselaer Writing Center:** http://www.rpi.edu/web/writingcenter/

- **The KidPub Children's PublishingCenter:** http://www.kidpub.com/

Now you want to place these into a section of your bookmarks file and add other bookmarks on this topic later. Here is what you do:

Bring up the **Edit Bookmarks** option in your browser. Create a new folder by selecting "**New**" under the **File Menu**:

Give the folder an appropriate name: for example, "English & Reading sites." Now drag the icons for all five sites, one at a time, into the folder you just created. See below for an example of what this might look like in the Bookmark menu after a folder is created in this way:

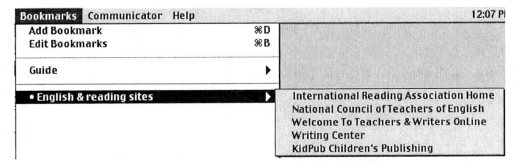

TRY THIS!

Section Four
Summary Exercises: Using Bookmarks

Exercises 4.1 – Review of New Terms and Concepts

_____ 1. Term for Bookmarks in *Internet Explorer*®

_____ 2. Menu you would use to get to the Edit Bookmarks option

_____ 3. Menu you use to make a new Folder for Bookmarks

_____ 4. This is what you create to organize Bookmarks under topics

_____ 5. What to do with Bookmark files besides organizing your own work

Exercises 4.2 – Practice Activities to Expand Your Skills

Try creating and organizing your own bookmark files for the following topics. Create a bookmark for each of the sites listed. Then create a folder with an appropriate name for each topic and drag in the bookmarks. (If any bookmarks don't work, try deleting the suffix and locating the information or report on the main site.)

Topic #1: Alternative Assessment Sites

• **Dr. Helen Barrett's Electronic Portfolios**
  http://electronicportfolios.com/

• **Kathy Schrock's Guide for Educators - Assessment Rubrics**
  http://school.discovery.com/schrockguide/assess.html

• **Rubric Creator Site by Rubistar**
  http://rubistar.4teachers.org/index.shtml

Topic #2: Digital Divide and Equity Reports

• **Digital Divide.org: Policy Solutions for the Digital Divide**
  http://www.digitaldivide.org/

• **The Growing Digital Divide (Hoffman and Novak, 2000)**
  http://www.markle.org/news/_news_pressreport_index.stm

• **Losing Ground Bit by Bit: Benton Foundation Report**
  http://www.benton.org/Library/Low-Income/home.html

FIVE – *Evaluating Internet Information*
How to Assess Web Site Quality

Why You Should be Careful

New Terms

- *Web page criteria*

- *Site map*

At a time when everything in the world seems so high-tech and highly-controlled, the Internet is, in some ways, a wild frontier. While there are oversight agencies that set up and monitor general items such domain designators (see p. 2 of this book), no one controls who posts web pages or the quality of their content.

Three kinds of problems arise from this lack of control. One of these, the hazards of offensive or dangerous subject matter or illegal activities, is dealt with in the next section (**SIX – Avoiding Internet Pitfalls**). The other two problems are less perilous but still have serious implications for teachers and students. Web pages can be less than useful for two reasons:

- **Content.** The Internet's vast information storehouse, unfortunately, contains some information that is incomplete, inaccurate, and/or out of date. It even has some sites that are works of complete fiction presenting themselves as fact.

- **Design.** We have learned a great deal in recent years about what makes a web site functional and easy to use. However, some sites are so poorly designed that people may find it difficult or impossible to locate and/or read the information they have to offer.

At the end of this chapter (p. 25), you will find criteria for evaluating web site quality, usefulness, and reliability. These criteria have been gleaned from several sources and are from Chapter 8 of *Integrating Educational Technology into Teaching* (Roblyer, 2003). Two of the categories (content and design) are described in more depth in this section.

Criteria for Evaluating Web Page Content

Students frequently accept as authoritative any information they find on the Internet. However, young people must learn that blind acceptance of any information (on the Internet or elsewhere!) is a risky practice. An essential skill for the Information Age is being able to evaluate information critically and look for the following signs that content is accurate and reliable:

- **Known author.** The web page author is a person or organization with a recognized name and authority. Be wary of those in which the author is not stated, whose credibility would be difficult to ascertain, or who have a known bias.

- **Contact information.** Authors of genuine sites usually give an e-mail address and/or other information one may use to contact them and ask questions about the content.

- **Frequent updates.** The site should list the last time the site was updated on the front page. Information has more credibility if the site is well-maintained.

- **References or links to other sites.** Some sites list documents they used as sources for the information. Others contain links to other sites one may use to verify statements and facts. Any information on a web page should be able to be authenticated by other sources.

You can help your students understand how important it is to confirm web site information by having them look at a site such as the following one and apply criteria for assessing information accuracy:

http://www.lme.mankato.msus.edu/newhartford/newhtfd.html

(HINT:
There is no such place as New Hartford, MN!)

Criteria for Evaluating Web Page Design

Another way to help verify the quality and accuracy of information on a web page is to look at its design. Web pages have more credibility if they are easy to use and have a professional-looking layout. Look for these characteristics to judge design quality:

- **Good structure and organization.** The first page of the site indicates clearly how to get to its various parts. Some sites do this with an option bar that appears at the top, bottom, or side of every page in the site. That way you can get easily to any part. See this example option bar from the U. S. DOE at: http://www.ed.gov/

Text or graphic links are clear. Branches are organized so that you can get back to the main page in no more than three clicks.

One device for large sites provides a link to a **site map** or an at-a-glance guide to the contents. (This was discussed briefly in Section 2 Exercises.) See the site map example below from the University of Maryland University College web site: http://umuc.edu

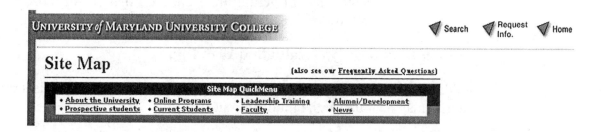

- **Visual design.** Pages are designed for good readability. There are a limited number of colors and fonts; fonts are easy to read, and colors are selected for contrast with the background. Graphics do not distract from reading the content. You can tell from looking at an icon the information you will get when you click it.

- **Easy navigation.** Pages load quickly. It's easy to get around in the site. Links are provided so you can get back to the main page from any part of the site. The most important information is given at the top of the page. All links work as they should. Larger sites have their own built-in search engine. See the example on the next page of the search engine at the U. S. House of Representatives web site at: http://thomas.loc.gov/

- **Miscellaneous.** Pages are short enough that each can be printed quickly. Video, sounds, and graphics help present the information, but pages provide alternate ways of getting the same information for those who lack advanced browser capabilities (e.g., frames).

More Information on Evaluating Web Pages

Additional information and links to web page evaluation checklists and rubrics may be found at the following sites:

Kathy Schrock's Guide for Educators – Collected links to web page evaluation rubrics and other assessment tools:

http://school.discovery.com/schrockguide/assess.html

Web Evaluation for Primary, Middle, and Secondary Grades – Three rubrics K–12 students can use to evaluate the quality of web sites.

http://www.siec.k12.in.us/~west/online/eval.htm

In addition, you can use the criteria checklist on the following page.

Web Page Evaluation Criteria and Tips
(from Chapter 8 of *Integrating Educational Technology into Teaching*, 3rd edition)

1.   **Content**
_____ All information is accurate. The "last time updated" date is given.
_____ Information is complete but not excessive or redundant.
_____ Information is well-organized and clearly labeled.
_____ Information is interesting, informative, and worthwhile.
_____ Information is not redundant to other sources; there is a reason to put it on the Web.
_____ All text has correct spelling, grammar, and punctuation.
_____ Level of content and vocabulary are appropriate for intended audience.
_____ Content is free from stereotyping, coarse or vulgar language, or matter that could be offensive to typical users.
_____ Author(s) of the page are clearly identified.
_____ The page gives an e-mail address or other way to contact authors.

2.   **Visual and Audio Design**
_____ The site has a consistent, common look and feel across pages.
_____ Graphics, animations, videos, and sounds make an important contribution.
_____ Pages have only one or two fonts.
_____ Each page uses limited numbers of colors, especially for text.
_____ Colors have been selected to be compatible with the *Netscape* 216-color palette.
_____ Type colors/styles and text-to-background contrast were selected for readability.
_____ Each graphic is designed to fit 640 x 480 pixel screens (allowing for scroll bars/toolbars).
_____ Each page is limited to 2 - 3 screens; the most important information is at the top.
_____ The pages are simply and attractively designed and make a user want to read them.

3.   **Navigation**
_____ Pages load quickly.
_____ Pages have simple, consistent navigation scheme for quick, easy navigation.
_____ The first page shows clearly how the site is organized and how to get to all items.
_____ Text and icon links are easy to identify. Graphics and sounds are clearly identified.
_____ Icons have been well-chosen to represent the information they link to.
_____ Each supporting page has a link back to the home page.

4.   **Miscellaneous (for larger sites and pages)**
_____ Requests for private information are secured.
_____ Page information is kept short enough that it can be printed quickly.
_____ Users can choose to load alternate versions of pages (e.g., text only, smaller images).
_____ The site has its own search engine for locating things within the pages.
_____ Branching is organized so all content is three clicks or fewer from the home page.

Use the following tips to make your sites and pages easier to design and use:

_____ Organize the site on paper ahead of time before inputting it to the computer.
_____ To speed loading, limit graphics to no more than 50K and re-use images whenever possible.
_____ Use GIFs for line art or graphics with limited colors and sharp edges; use JPEGs for photos with many colors and smooth gradients. Avoid PICT and other formats that must be converted by users.
_____ Test out your page in a real browser.
_____ Use a GIF spacer (1x1 transparent GIF) to space paragraphs, indents, or alignments on pages.

**Section Five
Summary Exercises: Evaluating Internet Information**

TRY THIS!

Exercises 5.1 – Review of New Terms and Concepts

_____ 1. One device on a web page that helps users by giving them an easy-to-read summary table of all links in the site

_____ 2. Larger sites need this built-in feature to help users find items on the site

_____ 3. One way you can tell a web site is accurate and reliable

_____ 4. How a well-designed web page should help users who may have limited browser capabilities (e.g., frames)

_____ 5. Another word for moving around in a web site

Exercises 5.2 – Practice Activities to Expand Your Skills

Try going to the following page of "spurious web sites." Using criteria you have learned from page 22 of this section, identify features about each of the following that allow you to tell they are spurious:

http://www.users.csbsju.edu/%7Eproske/evalwebp.html

• The True but Little–Known Facts About Women with Aids

_____

• A press release from Mattel Toys

_____

• An article in the *British Medical Journal*

_____

• California Crop Report

_____

• Psychosocial Parameters of Internet Addiction

_____

SIX – *Avoiding Internet Pitfalls*
How to Recognize and Prevent Problems

Types of Problems

As has been noted before, the Internet is a reflection of our society. This means that, like the world at large, there are some places on the Internet that pose potential dangers for those who venture on its paths. This does not mean people should avoid taking advantage of the Internet altogether, anymore than we should refrain from traveling because of the potential dangers of accidents or other threats. It does mean that educators and their students should be aware of the kinds of problems that can arise when they use the Internet and take steps to prevent them.

Five kinds of potential problem areas are discussed in this section. Also described are strategies that educators can use to make the Internet a safer, more worry-free place for teaching and learning.

Problem #1: Accessing Sites with Inappropriate Materials

Like a big-city bookstore, the Internet has materials that parents and teachers may not want students to see, either because they are inappropriate for an age level or because they contain information or images considered objectionable. Unfortunately, it is easy to access these sites unintentionally. For example, only three letters (the domain designator) differentiate the web site for our nation's Executive Branch (http://www.whitehouse.gov/) from one with X-rated images and materials.

Since it is so easy to access these sites without meaning to, classroom or lab Internet–usage rules do not safeguard against this problem. Most schools have found that the best way to prevent access to sites with inappropriate materials is to install **firewall** and/or **filtering software** on individual computers or on the school or district network that connects them to the Internet.

- **Filtering software.** An individual or a school can purchase and install these programs on one or more computers to limit user access to prohibited sites either on the basis of keywords, a list of off-limits sites, or a combination of these methods. Although there are many more on the market, review these sample sites:

    – *Cyber Patrol* (http://www.cyberpatrol.com)
    – *Cyber Sitter* (www.cybersitter.com /)
    – *Cybersnoop* (http://www.pearlsw.com)
    – *Net Nanny* (http://www.netnanny.com)
    – *Surf Watch* (http://www1.surfcontrol.com)
    – *WatchDog* (http://www.sarna.net/watchdog)
    – *X-Stop* (http://www.xstop.com)

Filtering programs also have other desirable features, such as keeping track of the time students spend on Internet sessions and reports of attempted site accesses. A site that can help teachers, parents, and others identify products to help meet various filtering needs is:

Get Net Wise: http://www.getnetwise.org/tools/

• **Firewall software.** These programs protect a computer from attempts by others to gain unauthorized access to it. Firewall software can be installed on individual computers but usually are part of a school or district network. Although the primary purpose of firewall software is to protect a computer from an outside attack, schools are finding that it also may prevent the user of the computer from *going* to a site. Therefore, it must be tailored to allow desired access.

Problem #2: Safety Issues for Students

Because they lack the experience that helps alert them to dangerous situations, young people are at special risk on the Internet in two different ways:

• **Online predators.** Young people tend to believe what they hear and read. Therefore, in a chatroom they may not consider the possibility that a 12-year-old named "Mary" may actually be a 50-year-old man.

• **Sales pitches aimed at children.** This is a problem similar to that posed by television commercials. Many Internet sites have colorful, compelling images that encourage people to buy. Young people may make commitments they cannot fulfill. Review another very helpful Internet site that addresses these issues. (See site on next page.)

http://www.safekids.com/child_safety.htm

This site has a document called *Safety on the Information Highway*, which was developed for the National Center for Missing and Exploited Children by newspaper columnist Lawrence J. Magid.

Kids' Rules for Online Safety

Magid says, "Teenagers are particularly at risk because they often use the computer unsupervised and because they are more likely than younger children to participate in online discussions regarding companionship, relationships, or sexual activity." He recommends teaching children a set of online rules. See the list of these rules at:

http://www.safekids.com/kidsrules.htm

Think of some ways you could teach these online rules to students.

For example,
you might have students create a multimedia presentation
of the rules listed above, or
you could have them role-play how they would react
if they encountered one of the problems Magid describes.

Problem #3: Fraud on the Internet

Teachers may find that the fastest, easiest way to order computer products and/or teaching materials is to go to a company's web site and order them online. However, most areas of the Internet are not secure. That is, what you do on the Internet can be monitored by others. Some people use this monitoring capability to look for a credit card number or other information they can use fraudulently.

As online consumers, teachers must be sure to purchase products only from well-known, reputable sites that offer a secure server. Secure servers have special programs to prevent outside monitoring of transactions. The URL for a secure server usually begins with "**https**" instead of the usual "**http**."

Problem #4: Computer Viruses

Viruses are programs written for malicious purposes. They come in several varieties and are named according to the way they work, e.g., worms, logic bombs, and Trojan horses. Two ways to get viruses on your computer from the Internet are through:

- **E-mail attachments with viruses.** An increasingly popular way to send files and programs to friends or colleagues is to attach them to e-mail messages. However, if a computer contains a virus that is programmed to attach itself to files, the virus can be sent inadvertently along with the file. When the person receiving the attachment opens it, the virus transfers to his/her computer.

- **Downloaded files and programs with viruses.** Procedures for transferring or downloading programs, documents, and other items from an Internet site to a computer are described in **Section Eight** of this book. As with e-mail attachments, viruses can attach themselves to files and programs and be received along with the item being downloaded.

What can you do to prevent these problems? Four procedures are recommended:

- **Keep virus–protection software up–to–date.** Always maintain, use, and keep updated a copy of a program designed to detect and safeguard against viruses.

- **Download only from reputable sites.** If you have never heard of or dealt with an organization before, downloading files from them can be risky. Shareware programs are a frequent source of attached viruses.

- **Never open e-mail attachments from unknown sources.** Be wary of e-mails from people or organizations you don't know, especially those with an eye-catching name like "Be sure you read this!" Do not open a suspicious e-mail or attachment before you confirm it has been sent for legitimate purposes.

- **Never open e-mail attachments until you confirm their origin.** Some viruses are programmed to send e-mails and attachments automatically through someone's e-mail program and to infect the computers of the recipients that open them. Even if you know the sender, be careful of opening attachments unless you are sure the person sent them intentionally.

Problem #5: Copyright Issues for Educators

The Internet is such a rich and easy-to-access source of documents, images, and other resources, it sometimes is easy to forget that many of these resources are copyrighted and protected by U. S. copyright laws.

To prevent problems, teach your students to look for copyright notices at the sites whose items you want to use. Then do the following:

- **If the site clearly is copyrighted**, contact the owners to request permission to use items.

- **If the site has no copyright statement,** be sure to reference the site by its URL and owner name on any materials you create with the resources.

Section Six
Summary Exercises: Avoiding Internet Pitfalls

Exercises 6.1 – Review of New Terms and Concepts

_____ 1. Software that protects a computer or network from viruses and other malicious attacks

_____ 2. Name for a program written for the specific purpose of doing harm to others' computers

_____ 3. What is said to be on a computer when software is in place to protect it from outside attacks

_____ 4. Key element in most of Magid's rules for children online

_____ 5. Software that is designed to keep users from going to specific sites uses either a list of prohibited URLs or this

Exercises 6.2 – Practice Activities to Expand Your Skills

1. **Update your security software** – Learn about the latest and best firewall and/or filtering software or download some free copies. Go to the following site and enter "Internet security" on its search engine: http://www.zdnet.com

2. **Tools for Families site** – Go to the GetNetWise site (http://www.getnetwise.org/tools) and follow procedures identified there for selecting a software that does the following:

   • Filters violence on a Windows NT computer for instant messaging, chats, e-mail, and the WWW
   • Monitors usage of any technology on a Macintosh computer

3. **Legal-use questions** – Let's say that you find an Internet site with a nice rubric you want to post on your own web site. You want it handy, so you don't want your students going to another URL for it. What procedure should you use in each of the following cases?

   a) The site has no copyright statement _____ _____

   b) The site has a label at the bottom of the first page that says: *Copyright 2003, M. D. Roblyer* _____

SEVEN – *Downloading and Using Images*
How to Obtain and Use Internet Graphics

New Terms

- *Download*
- *Image formats*
- *gif*
- *jpeg*
- *bmp*
- *eps*
- *pdf*
- *pict*
- *tif*

Why Images Are Important

The Internet has been around in text format since 1969. However, it became the society-wide phenomenon we know today only when the first web browser, *Mosaic*, made it possible for the Internet to appear on computer screens as images.

Why do images make such a difference? There may be two reasons. First, pictures are an "information shortcut." The old adage that "a picture is worth a thousand words" means that people grasp many concepts more quickly when they are presented as images rather than as text. Second, people seem able to remember a great deal of information visually.

But it is possible to take advantage of the visual tapestry of the Internet in ways other than receiving information. You can use your browser to "capture" or download any image you see from any web page and store it on your computer. Once you download an image, you can use it in a word–processing or desktop–publishing file, or even to create your own web pages.

How to Download Images

Let's say you wanted to have students use word processing to make an illustrated booklet of the three branches of the U. S. government. You might go to sites for each of these branches and capture images for them to use in their booklets.

Look at the following example. Several images appear on the White House web site for kids located at:

http://www.whitehouse.gov/kids

See a picture of this web site on the following page.

1777 flag

You can capture or download the image of the 1777 flag you see on this page. To "grab" an image from a web page is very simple, but the procedure differs slightly between Macintosh and Windows computers. To download the flag image, do the following:

• **On a Macintosh computer:** Click on the flag image, but instead of letting up the mouse after you click, hold it down until a menu like this one appears:

Downloading images in this way is a feature provided in your browser software.

| Back |
| Forward |
| Reload |
| Open this Page in Composer |
| Send Page... |
| Page Source |
| Page Info |
| Open this Link |
| Copy this Link Location |
| Add Bookmark for this Link |
| New Window with this Link |
| Save this Link as... |
| Open this Image |
| Copy this Image Location |
| **Save this Image as...** |
| Copy this Image |
| Load this Image |

Now drag down and select the "Save this image as..." option to save the image to your computer. See directions for what to do next after the Windows PC step (p. 35).

- **On a Windows PC**. Right-click on the flag image and, instead of letting up the mouse after you click, hold it down until a menu appears:

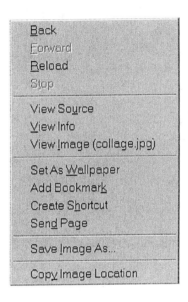

Now drag down and select "Save image as..." to save the image to your computer.

For either computer, after you select the "Save as" option, a box will appear to allow you to save the image on your computer. Depending on whether you have a Macintosh or PC computer, this box will look something like the following:

Save Image as:

1777.gif

The file name that will appear here will always be the name under which it was stored when it was put on the web page. The file name under which this flag image was stored is: 1777.jpg.

However, before you click "Save" to save the file, you can change this name to something you may find easier to remember. For example:

Save Image as:

flag.gif

Images on U. S. government web site are usually considered public domain and may be used without permission for educational purposes.

Downloading an image from the Internet is easy. But remember that many images you find on web pages are copyrighted, and their legal use is determined by copyright law and the owner of the web site. If you are not sure if you can use an image legally, contact the web site owner to request permission.

What to Do with Downloaded Images

After you save an image on your computer, you can insert it in documents or other web pages. However, you may need to change the **image format** from the original file format to another one.

Several image formats have been developed over the years to serve various purposes: either a certain computer or operating system required it, or certain formats deal better with differences among image types (e.g., photos rather than drawn images or clip art).

You can tell the format of an image by its suffix. For example, the flag was a **gif** file format. Images downloaded from web pages will be in one of the following formats:

- **gif** – Stands for "Graphics Interchange Format." Used for drawn images, illustrations, clip art, or animations.

- **jpeg** – Stands for "Joint Photographic Experts Group." Used for photographs.

If you want to use images to do your own web pages (see directions in **Section Eleven** of this booklet), they must be in one of these two formats.

There are several other types of image formats useful on computers. Some of the more common ones are listed below:

- **bmp** – Stands for "bitmapped." A standard format developed originally for use on DOS and Windows-compatible computers.

- **eps** – Stands for "Encapsulated Post Script." Developed to transfer artwork between any software packages that used PostScript printing files.

- **pdf** – Stands for "Portable Document Format." Used to store document pages as images. (See **Section Eight** of this booklet for more information on **pdf** files and software to read them.)

- **pict** – Short for "Picture" format, this was developed originally for use on Macintosh computers.

- **tif** – Stands for "Tagged Image File." Designed to be a flexible format for exchanging files among various software application and computers.

The user manual of each software package tells which image format it can take.

You can use images downloaded from web sites in several kinds of programs in addition to web page development, including:

- **Word processing** (e. g., *Microsoft Word*®),

- **Desktop publishing** (e. g., *Adobe PageMaker*®),

- **Presentation software** (e. g., *PowerPoint*®), and

- **Hypermedia authoring software** (e. g., *HyperStudio*®).

However, if you want to use images from the web in software packages that require formats other than **gif** or **jpg**, you may have to obtain and use an image manipulation software such as *Adobe Photoshop*® to save the image into another format.

TRY THIS!

Section Seven
Summary Exercises: Downloading Images

Exercises 7.1 – Review of New Terms and Concepts

_____ 1. Image format that animated graphics often are in

_____ 2. The first step in downloading an image from a web site on either a Macintosh or Windows PC platform

_____ 3. Sites from which you probably can use images for educational purposes without requesting permission

_____ 4. This determines the legal use of a copyrighted image

_____ 5. What you need to in order to save a downloaded image in an image format to use in another program

Exercises 7.2 – Practice Activities to Expand Your Skills

1. **Downloading Your Logo** – Say you want to do a *PowerPoint* presentation for your school or district. Go to your school or district web site and download its logo. Insert it on the title page of a *PowerPoint* presentation. Here is how it might look →

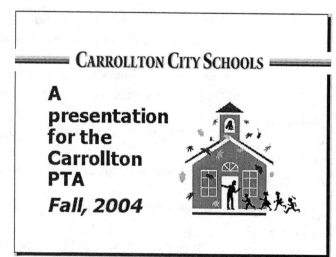

2. **Lesson Images** – Roblyer's *Integrating Educational Technology into Teaching* (2003) describes a lesson called "Selling a Space Mission." Students must do a persuasive *PowerPoint* presentation to gain funding for a hypothetical space mission. Here are web sites from which your students could obtain images for their presentations. Go to these sites and download some images they might find useful:

- **The NASA web site:** http://www.nasa.gov
- **The Dreamtime/NASA Partnership:** http://www.dreamtime.com
- **U.S. Space and Rocket Center:** http://www.spacecamp.com/

EIGHT – *Downloading Programs and Plug-ins*
How to Obtain Needed Web Resources

Kinds of Resources to be Downloaded

New Terms

- *plug-in*
- *pdf format*
- *streaming video*
- *streaming audio*

Web browsers made the Internet visual, but recent developments have given it sound and motion. Special programs called **plug-ins** have been created to allow people to see and hear these multimedia features that make the Internet increasingly life-like.

Although plug-ins tend to change and update rapidly, the Internet has a built-in way of allowing people to take full advantage of the Internet's multimedia features and keep up with advancements required for their use. Instead of buying the programs on disk or CD, Internet users can download many of them directly from the company site. This section describes some of the kinds you will need and procedures for downloading them.

Programs and Plug-ins You Will Need

- **Updated browser versions.** Most new computers come with a browser program stored on the hard drive. However, browsers change versions frequently. It is necessary to keep an up-to-date version in order to see newer Internet features. Download newer versions of browsers from the Netscape and Microsoft web sites:

 ®

Netscape Communicator® is available at:
http://www.netscape.com/

 ®

Internet Explorer® is available at:
http://www.microsoft.com/downloads/

- **Adobe *Acrobat*® viewer plug-in.** This program lets you see **pdf** (Portable Document Format) files. These are pages stored as images so they may be printed out with a page appearance identical to the original document. A **pdf** format is particularly important when the original text contains both print and images, or when one wants to see the appearance of the original document. For example, one might photograph and store the pages of the Declaration of Independence so history students could see them. Although the program to create **pdf** files must be purchased, the *Acrobat*® viewer plug-in required to see already-stored **pdf** files is available free from Adobe®, Inc at:

®

http://www.adobe.com/products/
acrobat/readstep.html

- **Streaming video and audio player plug-ins.** A new and exciting Internet capability is seeing action or hearing sounds live on the Internet. Streaming is so–called because it sends or "streams" images and sounds a little at a time so one need not download the files completely before using the contents. However, once these files are seen and stored on a computer, they also may be seen and/or heard later. *Real Player*® and *Real Audio*® are examples of these plug-ins.

Real Player® and *Real Audio*® are available at:

®

Real Networks.com
http://www.real.com/

- **Movie player plug-in.** Videos that have been digitized and stored as movie files may be viewed through a plug-in. One of the earliest, but still most useful, plug-ins for seeing these videos is the *QuickTime®* player available from the Apple Company. Although originally designed as a movie player, more recent versions of *QuickTime®* can also be used with streaming video and audio.

The *QuickTime®* player is available from:

Apple Computer, Inc.: **http://www.apple.com/**

How to Download Browsers and Other Programs

Downloading a program or plug-in is easy; simply go to the web site and follow the directions! Usually, the site provides very clear steps. Once you supply the information the site requests and click on the button to begin downloading, you will see a box similar to the following:

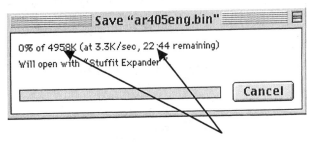

This box shows you how the download is progressing and approximately how much time is left before the download is complete. The downloading process usually places an icon for the program on your desktop. After the plug-in is downloaded, double-click on the icon to install the plug-in in the appropriate folder or directory. The program itself provides directions.

Section Eight
Summary Exercises: Downloading Programs and Plug-ins

TRY THIS!

Exercises 8.1 – Review of New Terms and Concepts

_____ 1. Documents in this format retain their original appearance when downloaded.

_____ 2. *Adobe Acrobat®*, *Real Player®*, and *Real Audio®* are examples of this kind of software.

_____ 3. Popular movie player available from Apple

_____ 4. What **pdf** stands for

_____ 5. *Real Player®* allows users to do this

Exercises 8.2 – Practice Activities to Expand Your Skills

Download the four plug-ins described below to your own computer. Try out each of them with the files indicated.

❶ *Adobe Acrobat®* at: **http://www.adobe.com/products/acrobat/readstep.html**

Now use this plug-in to look at the PDF versions of U. S. DOE reports such as *The Corporate Imperative: A Business Guide for Implementing Strategic Education Partnerships* available at: **http://www.ed.gov/pubs/strategicpartner/**

❷ *Real Player®* and
❸ *Real Audio®* at: **http://www.real.com/**

Now use the *Real Audio®* plug-in to listen to current news stories on National Public Radio at: **http://www.npr.org/**

❹ *QuickTime®*: **http://www.apple.com/**

Now use this plug-in to look at *QuickTime®* movies related to education available from Apple at: **http://ali.apple.com/events/aliqttv/**

NINE – *Internet Troubleshooting*
How to Recognize and Address Common Errors

Three Kinds of Errors

Like most technologies, the Internet presents its share of "head scratchers." The majority of these errors and problems can be corrected easily; others require more complicated "fixes" or adjustments. Three of the most common difficulties for Internet users are:

- **Site connection failures.** After you enter the URL, the site won't come up on the screen.

- **Site features won't work.** The animation, movie, or sound file on the site will not work.

- **Memory errors.** The computer or the browser does not have enough Random Access Memory (RAM) to load a site or use a plug-in.

Problem ❶: A Site Won't Connect

This is the most common problem people encounter, and it may occur for any of several reasons. The error message for each problem indicates the cause.

- **URL syntax errors.** As mentioned in Section One of this book, each dot and letter in a URL has to be correct, or the site won't load. The most common error message for this problem is: ". . . unable to locate the server. Please check the server name and try again." If this message appears, check the URL syntax and make sure you have not done any of the following:

  - Confused the letter "l" with the number "1"
  - Confused the letter "O" with the number "0"
  - Confused the hyphen "-" with the underline "_"
  - Confused forward slash "/" with backward slash "\" in the "http://" or in suffixes
  - Omitted a required punctuation mark
  - Misspelled a part of the URL
  - Used the wrong domain designator (e.g., "edu" instead of "org")

Many URL errors occur in suffixes that follow the domain designator. Try omitting all suffixes beyond the slash and going directly to the main part of the URL. The main page may show the links you want, or the site may have a built-in search engine you can use.

- **Local or domain server down.** If you have checked the URL syntax and are positive it is correct, it may be that the server that hosts the web site is not working temporarily. It may have a technical problem or simply may be down for regular maintenance. In this case, you may get an error message like the one shown previously. Wait for a day or two and try it again.

  A rarer cause of connection failures is that the server handling Internet traffic for the network or for users in the geographic region is not working properly. Error messages say "Failure to resolve domain error. Try this site again later" or "Page has no content."

- **Bad or dead links.** If a URL repeatedly fails to connect and you are sure the syntax is correct, the site may have been taken off the Internet. This is a **bad or dead link**. If this is the case, you may get the same error message given previously or the site may provide a message that says "bad link."

- **Firewalls.** Sometimes a site will not connect because a network's firewall blocks it. (See **Section Six** of this book.) If you think your network's firewall is blocking your access to a site in error, contact your network administrator and request that this be adjusted.

Problem ❷: Internet Features Won't Work

If an Internet site indicates that it has a special feature such as an animation, movie, or sound but it will not work for you, there are three possible causes:

- **Plug-in required.** It may be that your computer does not have the special program or plug-in required to play the movie or sound. Usually, if a special plug-in is needed, the site will have a link to where you can go to download the plug-in and install it on your computer. (See **Section Eight** on Downloading Programs and Plug-ins.)

- **Compatibility errors.** The Internet works because there are agreements in place about how to make various machines and programs "talk" to each other. However, sometimes there are differences between operating systems or versions of software that make them incompatible. Some sites can be seen only with *Netscape*; some only with *Internet Explorer*. The web page usually indicates if it requires a specific browser.

- **Programming errors.** Internet web pages usually are written in a combination of three programming languages: HyperText Markup Language (HTML), Java, and less often, Perl. HTML is the basic language that sets up and formats a page, Java is used for special features like counters or chatrooms, and Perl is used to write "CGI scripts," which are used when the site wants people to enter information into the web page (e.g., a survey).

If you get a Javascript error message, make sure Java is enabled (select **Preferences** under the **Edit Menu)** and/or download a newer version of Java. (See **Section Eight** on Downloading Programs and Plug-ins.) If you have an enabled, up-to-date version but still get a Javascript error message, it may be that there really is an error in the Java or Perl language of the program or script. In this case, the only thing you can do is to contact the site and alert them to the error.

Problem ❸: Out-of-Memory Error Messages Appear

In addition to the problems described above, you may get errors because your computer or the program lacks the memory required to see the images at the site or to run the plug-in. On a Macintosh, you may get an error message that says you have insufficient memory or the site may keep trying to load indefinitely. If this occurs, try allocating more memory to the browser. On the Macintosh, click once on the program icon for the browser and select "**Get Info**" from the **File Menu**. When the Information box appears, click on **Show: Memory** and enter larger numbers in the boxes.

Section Nine
Summary Exercises: Internet Troubleshooting

Exercises 9.1 – Review of New Terms and Concepts

_____ 1. A URL that has worked in the past fails to connect over a period of days. Error message says it cannot find the site. What is the likely problem?

_____ 2. You enter the your school district URL. An error message says it cannot find the server. What should you do?

_____ 3. The site has an icon labeled "Play movie." You click on it, but nothing happens. What should you do?

_____ 4. You enter a URL for a site and get an error message that says "You are not permitted access to this site." What is the likely problem?

_____ 5. There is an online survey you would like to complete, but the survey will not allow you to enter anything. What is a possible problem?

Exercises 9.2 – Practice Activities to Expand Your Skills

Spot the errors in the following URLs that would result in an error message. Correct them and go to the site to make sure they work:

1. http://www.psuedu _____

2. http//www.iste.org_____

3. http://www.app1e.com ____ _____ _____

4. http://www.animfactory.com/af-animals-bears-page-aa.html

_____

5. http://www.quotationspage.c0m/ _____

TEN – *Integrating the Internet into Teaching Strategies, Resources, and Lesson Links*

New Terms

- *tele-mentoring*
- *e-pals*
- *keypals*
- *electronic field trip*
- *virtual field trip*
- *social action project*

Powerful Teaching and Learning Strategies

Now that you have learned how to be a skilled Internet traveler, you can begin using its wealth of resources to enrich your teaching. This section provides information to help you start integrating the Internet into your classroom activities.

The following are models of how to integrate the Internet into classroom activities in many content areas. Go to the URL for each lesson and think about how you might adapt the strategy for you own uses. (**Section Eleven** shows you how to design your own web site to support online activities.)

Strategy #1: Electronic Penpals (E-pals or Keypals)

- **How People Live in Europe and the Middle East.** Kids in the U.S. e-mail their contemporaries in other countries to ask questions about the European countries that they will be studying. **http://www.kidlink.org/KIDPROJ/Euro/**

- **Math Penpals.** Students communicate with their "math penpals" on a variety of topics that have mathematical themes, e.g., weather data (daily high/low temperatures, weekly precipitation) will be shared weekly. Monthly events include surveys and comparison pricing. **http://www.kidlink.org/KIDPROJ/Math/**

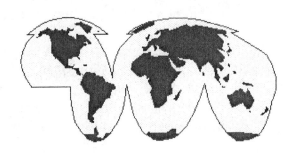

Strategy #2: Individual and Cooperative Research Projects

- **Chewing the Fat and Other Novel Expressions.** Students in paired schools in England and New Zealand research each other's use of slang.
  http://www.interlink.org.nz/projects/chewfat/ chewfat2.html

- **Global Wildlife Migration Study.** As students track the journeys of a dozen migratory species each spring, they share their own field observations with classrooms across the hemisphere.
  http://www.learner.org/jnorth/

**Migratory bird on the
Smithsonian National Zoo Web Site.
Photo available at: http://natzoo.si.edu/**

- **Tooth Tally Project.** In this project, losing a tooth becomes a teachable moment. As first graders in various locations compare how many teeth they lose, they practice counting skills, collect data, and learn to make and interpret graphs.
  http://wilburnes.wcpss.net/tooth01.htm

Strategy #3: Electronic Mentoring

- **Telementoring Young Women in Science, Engineering, and Computing.** Program funded by the National Science Foundation to provide online communities of support for young women taking technical courses in high school.
  http://www.edc.org/CCT/telementoring/index2.html

National Science Foundation
WHERE DISCOVERIES BEGIN

- **The History of Spanish Texas.** A 4th grade teacher asks members of a university electronic forum to give her students information on the Spanish explorers.
  http://riceinfo.rice.edu/armadillo/Projects/letters.html

- **Ask an Expert.** This site provides links to people who have volunteered their time to answer questions and web pages that provide information on various topics.
  http://www.askanexpert.com/

Strategy #4: Electronic (Virtual) Field Trips

- **Lots of Bread.** In this field trip about bread baking, students learn about nutrition and do science labs to explore principles at work in bread-making processes.
  http://www.field-guides.com/sci/bake/index.htm

- **Field Trips International.** Many teachers take their students on field trips in their local community. This site allows teachers and students to document their field trip and share it with others around the world.
  http://www.gsn.org/project/fieldtrips/

- **My America Virtual Field Trip.** Students are guided by a set of four questions as they tour selected sites: What does America mean to you? If you are an American citizen, what does it mean to you to be American? What are some of the privileges Americans have which are lacking in other parts of the world? Who were the first people living in the United States?
  http://www.field-guides.com/ss/america/index.htm

- **Impressionists**. Students explore impressionism by taking a virtual tour of five impressionist paintings, and exploring techniques (theme, color, and brushwork) artists used to create their masterpieces.
  http://www.biography.com/impressionists/

Strategy #5: Group Development of Products

- **Global Warming**. Student teams collaborate to decide whether or not to support a piece of legislation that would decrease the emissions of greenhouse gases by 20% by the year 2005. After online research, they prepare a multimedia position statement.
- **http://students.itec.sfsu.edu/ITEC815/antaramian/**

- **MusicLand Theme Park.** Students become a team of designers assigned to build a new music theme park in their city. It will have different "Lands" for each of several musical genres. Each design team chooses a musical genre to research and decide on a definitive time period and appropriate location for the genre.
  http://www.itdc.sbcss.k12.ca.us/curriculum/
  musicland.html

- **Personal Trainer.** Students become personal trainers employed by a fitness consulting firm that provides individualized diet and exercise portfolios. They are assigned a client and develop a weekly exercise program and menus that will fit into the person's lifestyle.
  http://www.itdc.sbcss.k12.ca.us/curriculum/
  personaltrainer.html

- **The Real Scoop on Tobacco.** Students become experts about tobacco and issues surrounding its use. They create an attention-getting music video, skit, or TV commercial that visually conveys the message that kids shouldn't smoke.
  http://www.itdc.sbcss.k12.ca.us/curriculum/tobacco.html

- **Weather Scrapbook.** Students research the weather topics and create a presentation of their findings with *Microsoft PowerPoint* or *FrontPage*. They learn how to put together their own multimedia weather scrapbook.
  http://www.educationcentral.org/stormy/main.htm

OUR SEAS AND OUR SKIES

OF EXCELLENCE AT NOAA

From the National Oceanographic and Atmospheric Administration (NOAA) at: http://www.noaa.gov/

Strategy #6: Social Action Projects

- **Save the Beaches.** Students pick trash on their local beaches, analyze it, and collaborate online with other sites to develop ways to prevent beach pollution.
  http://www.swindsor.k12.ct.us/Schools/tems/beaches/index.html

- **Teen Court.** This volunteer organization was established to give youth offenders a chance to clear their arrest from their permanent record by performing community service and other duties ordered by the court. All teens admit their guilt and agree to accept a sentence given to them by a jury of their peers. (A judge is present.)
  http://www.thinkquest.org/library/
  lib/site_sum_outside.html?tname=2640&url=2640/

For more ideas and information on how to integrate the Internet into curriculum, see: M. D. Roblyer's *Integrating Educational Technology into Teaching* (Prentice Hall, 2003).

```
 TRY THIS!
```

Section Ten
Summary Exercises: Integrating the Internet into Teaching

Exercises 10.1 – Review of New Terms and Concepts

_____ 1. Another word for providing students with online mentors to guide their learning

_____ 2. An online "journey" students may take to a location to which they would not ordinarily be able to travel

_____ 3. A person with whom one may exchange correspondence by e-mail

_____ 4. Online projects designed to focus students on developing answers for social problems and issues

_____ 5. Organization whose web site is: http://www.kidlink.org

Exercises 10.2 – Practice Activities to Expand Your Skills

The following are three groups of sites with lesson plans and other materials you can use to develop your own Internet-based teaching and learning strategies. Enter some or all of these links into your browser and create bookmarks for each site as you connect to it. Create a folder for each group, or create folders for your own categories of links. (See **Section Four** of this book for help on using bookmarks.) Look for lesson plans, strategies, and resources that will be of particular use to you in teaching your content area.

Internet Lesson Plans and Teaching Resources

- **The Blue Web 'n Library** – A compilation of hundreds of links to prize-winning lesson and resource sites at:
  http://www.kn.pacbell.com/wired/bluewebn

- **High Plains Regional Technology Consortium** – A collection of lessons and teacher resources at: **http://4teachers.org/intech/lessons/**

- **KIDPROJ** – A site that sponsors ongoing technology projects for kids to join at: **http://www.kidlink.org/KIDPROJ/index.html**

- **The Apple Learning Exchange** – Lesson plans available from the Apple Computer, Inc. at: **http://ali.apple.com/**

- **The ThinkQuest Internet Challenge** – School winners of the ThinkQuest competitions to design web-based learning projects at: **http://www.thinkquest.org**

- **The WebQuest Page** – Site of teacher-and-student-designed webquest projects hosted by San Diego State University at: **http://edweb.sdsu.edu/webquest/webquest.html**

- **Virtual Field Trips Site** – Lists of annotated virtual field trips on nature topics with additional teacher's resources for each of the trips. **http://www.field-guides.com**

Content Area Lessons and Other Resources for Teachers

- **Discovery.com** – A searchable bank of lessons plans on all subject areas maintained by the Discovery Channel's web site at: **http://school.discovery.com/lessonplans/**

- **Microsoft Lesson Connection** – A searchable database of lesson plans maintained by Microsoft at: **http://www.k12.msn.com/LessonConnection/Teacher.asp**

- *The New York Times* – A searchable bank of lesson ideas maintained by *The New York Times* at: **http://www.nytimes.com/learning/teachers/lessons/archive.html**

- **Smithsonian Institute** – Lesson plans and other teaching resources on a variety of topics maintained by the Smithsonian at: **http://educate.si.edu/**

- **United Nations** – Teaching modules, classroom activities, and on-going events to help teach global issues: Human Rights, Health, Land Mines, Environment, Women, and Poverty at:
  http://www.un.org/Pubs/CyberSchoolBus/

- **U. S. DOE** – A searchable bank of lesson activities and other resources maintained by the U.S. DOE at:
  http://www.ed.gov/free/subject.html

Sites to Help with Collaboration Among Schools

- **"World's Largest" Keypal Locator service** – This site links up students from all over the world to work together and exchange information on topics of mutual interest.
  http://www.epals.com/

- **The Global SchoolNet Foundation** – A site of examples of past collaborative projects and information on how to join current ones at:
  http://www.gsn.org/pr/index.html

- **Web–Assistance Site.** University of Minnesota site to help K – 12 educators learn how to set up their own Internet servers, link K – 12 educators and students at various sites, and help them find and use K – 12 web resources. **http://web66.umn.edu/**

ELEVEN – *CREATING YOUR OWN WEB SITE*
How to Create New Pages and Adapt Existing Ones

Why You May Want Your Own Web Site

New Terms

- HTML editor
- *Netscape Composer®*
- upload
- FTP
- table
- index page
- story-board

The Internet is becoming an increasingly common way for people to communicate. Just as sending e-mails is becoming as commonplace as telephone calls to contact individuals, posting web pages is becoming an accepted strategy for delivering information and/or working with many people at the same time.

In education, teachers are using web pages to:

- **Communicate information to parents, students, and others on a continuing basis** – Web-based newsletters and flyers can take the place of paper ones. Also, some schools are beginning to post (password protected) student progress reports so parents can track this important information.

- **Structure and carry out lessons** – Many of the learning strategies described in **Section Ten** of this book require a web site. A site may serve a variety of purposes, depending on the type of lesson. Sometimes teachers have students create their own web site as part of a learning activity.

What You Need to Create Your Own Web Site

You can use two different strategies to create your own "web presence." These include:

- **Creating pages from scratch** and linking them, or

- **Downloading or "grabbing" existing pages** and modifying them for your own use.

This section will show you how to use each of these methods to develop your own personal web site.

For either of these strategies, you will need **three** different resources in order to create your web site:

You can download and pre-view both free and fee-based FTP and web page develop-ment software at: http:// download. cnet.com

FTP is also a verb! You use FTP software to FTP your files to the server.

❶ **Web development software** – Although you can create pages by programming them in HTML code, teachers will find that using an *HTML editor* (i.e., web page development software) is preferable; it is easier, faster, and requires much less technical skill.

As with most tool software, web page development software packages vary considerably as to features and prices. Packages such as Microsoft *FrontPage* and Macromedia *Dreamweaver* are full-featured and must be purchased. However, other more basic software is available free or as a free component of another software package. One of the latter, *Netscape Composer*®, is a built-in web page development software component of the browser *Netscape Communicator*®.

In this book, we use *Netscape Composer*® to illustrate how to develop web pages. If you don't have the software, you can download it free from this site:

http://home.netscape.com/download/

❷ **File Transfer Protocol (FTP) software** – After developing all the pages of your site, you must transfer or upload them to a server. To do this, you need *FTP* software. If your web site will be housed on your school or district server, technical personnel there may provide an FTP package or they may want to upload your pages for you. If your site will be on another server, contact the web administrator to find out required procedures.

❸ **Server to house the web site** – Your web site must have a "home," that is, a computer or server on which it resides. Most teachers choose to have their web site on their school or district server. If so, you may want to find out the procedures that have been established in your school or district for obtaining required permissions and for uploading pages to the server.

A Few Caveats When Creating Web Page Information

Before you begin developing pages, consider these items:

- **Limit sharing of personal information** – Since so many people will have access to your web site, you may wish to limit personal information such as pictures and telephone numbers. Most teachers include only an e-mail address.

- **Limit photos and large graphics** – These take a long time to load and can be frustrating to users (e.g., parents) who wish to see the information on your site.

- **Address web page criteria** – Use the same criteria for your own page that you wish to see in other sites. Review criteria for effective web pages on page 25 of this book. You may want to select other teacher sites you like and follow their structure.

A Suggested Development Sequence: Eight Phases

In *Integrating Educational Technology into Teaching*, Roblyer (2003) recommends a sequence of eight phases to successfully developing a web page or web site:

Inspiration (Inspiration Software, Inc.) is a useful software for creating a plan for the structure of your web site and showing how the pages link together.

Phase 1: Plan and storyboard – Planning and design are the most difficult, important—and most frequently neglected—first steps in developing a web site. Though most people want to get to the fun of development, planning is critical to a well-designed web site. Storyboard (i.e., make a rough sketch of) a plan for the site by using cognitive mapping software or 3" x 5" sticky notes placed on large pieces of poster board to represent the web pages.

Phase 2: Develop pages with text – The next step is to create blank web pages and insert text elements such as titles, paragraphs of description, and any text labels that will later serve as links. There are three kinds of page structures: basic, basic with anchors on the page, and frames. (This section focuses on designing basic pages.)

Phase 3: Insert images and sounds – Pictures, animations, and movies come next. Images and animations must be in GIF or JPEG format; movies and sounds must be in MPEG format. (See **Section Seven** for information on various formats for graphic images.) If movies or audio are to be streamed, the page should inform the user and provide a way to obtain the plug-in needed to see or hear the item (See **Section Eight**.)

Phase 4: Insert links and frames – After all pages are designed, insert links or "hot spots" from text and images to other pages in the site and locations on the Internet.

Phase 5: Insert interactive elements – If desired, make the web page "interactive" by inserting Java applets, CGI scripts, and mail-to commands to gather comments from users who visit your site.

Phase 6: Test in a browser – Many development programs have a built-in preview system, but it is essential to test the site with an actual browser to observe how it will work when it is published on the Web.

Phase 7: Publish (upload) the site – For others to see created web pages, developers must place them on a server. This is called publishing the site. If the user can sit down at the keyboard of the computer acting as the server, the files may be moved over from a disk to the hard drive. For servers that are not nearby, the user may upload the pages to the server as FTP files.

Phase 8: Gather evaluation comments, revise, and maintain the site – The best web sites are those that are updated regularly based on user comments and the continuing insights of the developers. This may be done through CGI programs built into the page (See Phase 5 above) or simply through inviting e-mailed comments.

Next, try an exercise in building your own page. In this exercise, you will be creating a web site like the one at the following URL. Go to this sample site first and see what you will be creating:
http://www.prenhall.com/startingout

Step 1: Starting the First Page

To obtain a blank *Netscape Composer*® page, load *Netscape Communicator*® and select **New – Blank Page** from the **File Menu.**

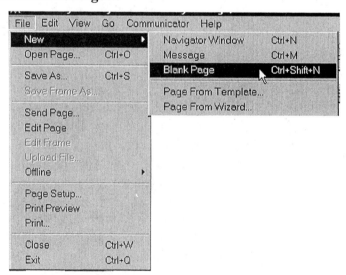

Set a name and background color by selecting **Page Colors and Properties** from the **Format Menu**:

If you want to use a pattern or an image for your background instead of a color, click the Image box instead of the Background box, and choose an image file stored on your hard drive.

• Click the **General Tab**; type "index.html" for the title.

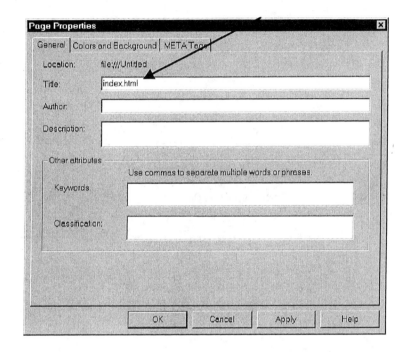

• Click the **Colors and Background** tab (see example, next page); click the **Use custom colors** button; click the **Background** box. Color options will appear; click on white for the background color. Click **OK** to confirm the choices and return to the page. Select **Save As** from the **File Menu** and save the page under the name: **index.html**

Note that you can select Color, Alignment, Size, and other formatting options from the Format Menu, as well as from the **Format Toolbar**.

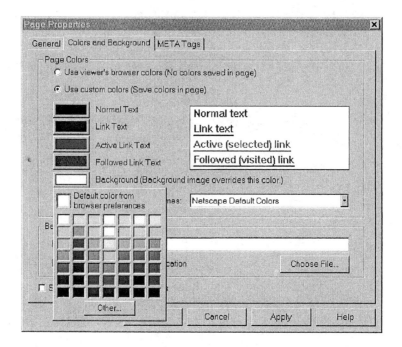

Step 2: Inserting and Formatting Text

Click on the page and type a title and a welcome like the one shown in the example below:

G.L. Branch's Home Page

Welcome to my page!
Click on one of the links below to learn about me.

- After you type the text as shown, format it. First, highlight it by dragging your mouse across it.

- On the **Format Toolbar**, click the arrow beside the **Text Color** box and drag down to select a text color.

- On the **Format Toolbar**, select **Font Size** and enter 18 for the size.

- On the **Format Toolbar**, click the **Alignment** icon and drag down to select **Centered**.

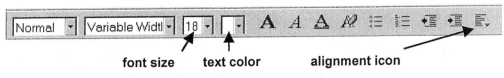

font size   text color   alignment icon

Before you insert any images, all should be saved as gif or jpeg format and placed in the same directory or folder on your hard drive as the pages.

Step 3: Inserting Graphics

Thousands of free and inexpensive graphics are available for your use in your web pages. Here are some sites to peruse in search of just the right image or background:

- **List of links to graphics sites:** http://www.free-graphics.com

- **Microsoft's graphics site:** http://dgl.microsoft.com

- **Graphics, buttons, bullets, rules, and animations:** http://www.belsnwhistles.com

- **Collection of free and for-a-fee animated graphics:** http://www.animfactory.com

If you want to use the tree image shown in the example for this exercise, go to the example web site (**http://www.prenhall.com/startingout**) and download it using the steps described in **Section Seven**.

- When you have an image that you want to insert from your hard drive, first click on the area of the page where you want it to appear. In this example, click just to the left of the "G. L. Branch" title and make a space above the text for the tree image by pressing Enter or Return to bring the text down several lines.

- Select **Image** from the **Insert Menu,** and click on **Choose File.** Select the tree image (or another image you want to insert) from the hard drive; click **OK**.

- Double-click on the tree image OR select **Image Info** from the **Format Menu.** Click on the **Paragraph tab,** select **Center** alignment by clicking on the **Center** radio button, and click **OK**.

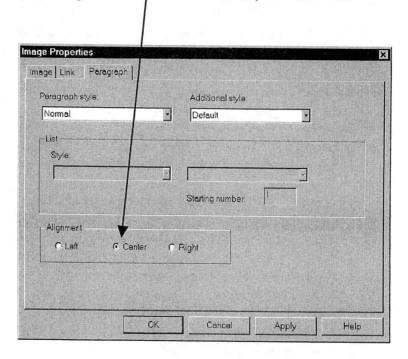

Now the page should look like the example on the next page.

G.L. Branch's Home Page

Welcome to my page!
Click on one of the links below to learn about me.

Step 4: Inserting Tables

In a word processing document, you can use tabs to space text items evenly across a page. In an HTML page, you must insert a *table* and place the text in its cells. To create the set of labels you see in the example below (which will later become links to other pages), do the following:

- Click just below the text you have inserted and select **Table** from the **Insert Menu**.

- Enter "1" for the number of Rows and "4" for the number of columns.

- Click the **Center** radio button for **Alignment**. Click **OK.**

- Click inside each cell in the Table and enter the words shown in the example. **DO NOT** press Enter or Return after typing a word in a cell. Either click inside another cell or click outside the table. The table should look like this:

Personal	Professional	My School

Step 5: Creating Additional Pages

A web site typically consists of several pages. The one in the example we are creating here has three:

- **A home page** (the **index.html** page you just created)

- **A personal page:** See example on page 65.

- **A professional page:** See example on page 66.

Web pages can be saved with either the "html" or the "htm" suffix.

Create the text of each page by using the procedures described in Steps 1 through 3. You can either make these pages look like the examples shown here, or you can experiment with your own text and graphics.

Be sure to **Save** each of the pages (in the same folder as the "index.html" page) as: **mypersonalpage.htm** and **myprofpage.htm**. (We will use these names to make links in Step 6.)

On each page, create only the text, not the Table below it. We will insert Tables in Step 6 (page 67).

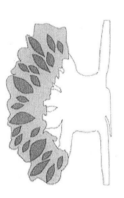

G.L. Branch's Personal Page

My background - I am originally from Cumberland, Maryland. I am married and have two children. I have the following degrees:

- B.A. in English/Secondary Education from the University of Maryland, College Park
- M.Ed. (online) from the University of Maryland University College (UMUC), Adelphi

My interests and hobbies - I enjoy spending time with my family and doing the following activities:

- I work one weekend a month with other volunteers for Habitat for Humanity. This year we built a house for a family in our community.
- I like to travel and take photographs of the places we visit. I always digitize the photographs and make them into an online "album" so I can share them easily with my students and friends.

My work - I am a fifth grade teacher at the Neuwave Elementary School. Learn more about my work by visiting my Professional page (see link below).

HOME	Professional	My School

Click here to e-mail me

G.L. Branch's Professional Page

Teaching Experience - I have been a Teacher for 14 years and have loved every minute (well, most minutes!) of it. Here is where I have taught:

- The Green Montessori School - Potomac, Maryland
- Excelsior Elementary School - Fresno, California
- Neuwave Elementary School - Albany, New York

Teaching Specialties - I am especially proud of the following recent accomplishments:

- Writing across the curriculum - I have developed some great lessons to encourage my students to write in science, social studies, and other areas. (E-mail me if you want to get a copy.)
- Workshops for teachers - I have developed and given workshops on how to use digital cameras and digitized images in teaching various topics and how to develop your own web site.

Favorite Links - Here are a few of my favorite sites. Click on each one to go there:

- Electronic Portfolios
- Blue Web'n Lesson Plans Site
- M. D. Roblyer Textbook
- ISTE Site

Personal   HOME   My School

Click here to e-mail me

Step 6: Inserting Links Between Pages

To link all your pages together to make a web site, make the labels in the Table into links in the following way:

- Go back to the **index.html** page and highlight the "Personal" label in the first cell of the table.

- Select **Link** from the **Insert Menu**. Under the Link tab, type **mypersonalpage.htm** in the URL line as shown below. Click OK.

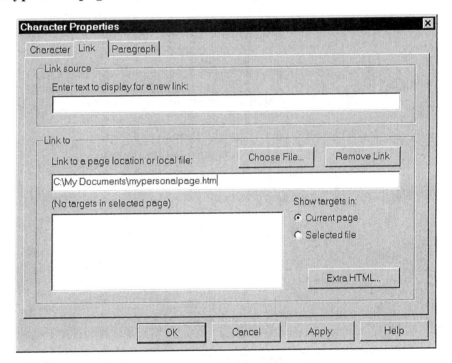

- Now highlight the "Professional" label in the next cell. Again, select **Link** from the **Insert Menu**. Under the Link tab, type **myprofpage.htm** in the URL line as shown below. Click OK.

- Highlight the **My School** label and follow the same procedure. However, for this name, put a URL instead of a page name. You can either put the following URL (the one for the author's university web site) or the URL of your own school: **http://www.umuc.edu**

- Insert this **Table** of links on each of the other two pages in this way. Choose **Select Table** from the **Edit Menu**. Then select **Copy** from the **Edit Menu**. Go to **mypersonalpage.htm**, click below the text on the page and select **Paste** from the **Edit Menu**. The table should appear there.

- However, since the page you are on now *is* the Personal page, you don't need a link to it in the Table of links. Highlight the "Personal" label and change it to read "HOME" instead. Highlight the "HOME" label, select **Link** from the **Insert Menu**, and change the link to "index.html" to link it to the Home page

- Follow the same procedure for inserting and modifying the links on the "myprofpage.htm" page. This time you'll change the "Professional" label to read "HOME" and change the link to "index.html".

Step 7: Inserting Links Within a Page

You may want to have links to other sites in your pages. Also, you will want to include an e-mail address that users can click on to bring up a message page in their e-mail software. Practice inserting both kinds of links on the "myprofpage.htm."

- On the section of Favorite Links, highlight the text that says "M. D. Roblyer Textbook." Select **Link** from the **Insert Menu**. Insert the following URL and click OK: **http://www.prenhall.com/roblyer**

- Follow the same procedure for the other links. Insert the following URL's and then re-save your page:

  – **Electronic Portfolios:** http://electronicportfolios.com/

  – **Blue Web'n Lesson Plans Site:**
    http://www.kn.pacbell.com/wired/bluewebn/

  – **ISTE Site:** http://www.iste.org

- Insert a line of text below the **Table** of links: "Click here to e-mail me." Highlight it and select **Link** from the **Insert Menu**. Insert the following:

mailto:*YOUR E-MAIL ADDRESS HERE*

Step 8: Previewing Pages in a Browser

Although your pages may look fine in *Netscape Composer*®, always test them in a "live" browser to see how they will look on the Internet. Before you do this step, make sure you have saved each of your pages:

- Be sure you are connected to the Internet and have all three pages open in *Netscape Composer*®. From the **File Menu**, select **Page – Open.** Click the **Navigator** radio button.

- Click "Choose file" and choose from your computer the name of the page you want to preview. Type "index.html" to preview this page. Click on all links to make sure they work. If there are errors, correct them and save the changes.

- To see your changed document, you will need to click "reload" in your browser.

- "Mailto" is an HTML command that indicates an e-mail address follows. When you insert your own e-mail address, it creates a link that brings up your e-mail address in the user's default e-mail program.

Open Page   ☒

Enter the World Wide Web location (URL) or specify the local file you would like to open:

| C:\My Documents\index.html | Choose File... |

Open location or file in: ○ Composer
                           ● Navigator   [Open]   [Cancel]   [Help]

Step 9: Uploading to a Server

The most technical step in developing a web site is to use an FTP software package to transfer (upload) the page files you have created to a server (computer) on which they will reside.

Most schools or districts that have their own server also have their own FTP software and procedures they want you to follow for uploading new files. However, if you are using another site (e.g., one made available to you by your ISP), you will need to contact the web administrator of that server for usernames and passwords required for you to FTP files.

You will need a directory or folder in which all your page files and graphics will be stored. If one does not already exist on the server, the web administrator will need to create one for you. On the next page is an example of one such package: the *WS_FTP* program (Ipswitch, Inc). All FTP programs have the same basic steps: (a) connect with the server, (b) highlight files to be transferred from your disk or hard drive, and (c) click an arrow to transfer them. However, procedures to accomplish these will look slightly different in each software.

Remember that you will not be able to do Steps 9 and 10 here unless you have a server to which you can upload. Also, if you need an FTP software package, you can download a package from the following web site:

http://download.cnet.com

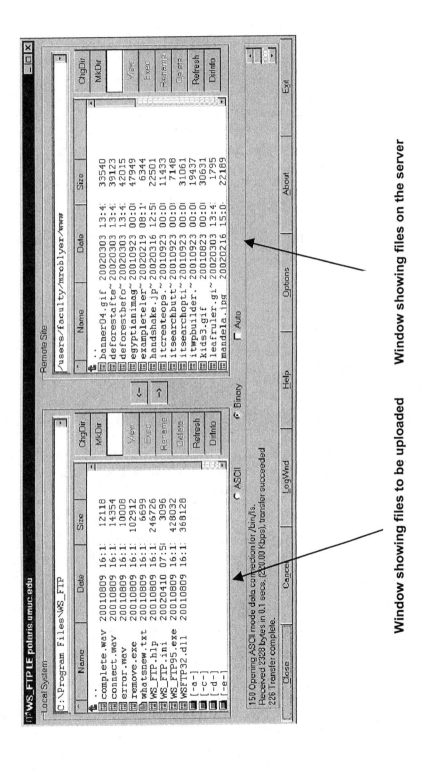

Window showing files to be uploaded   Window showing files on the server

Step 10: Using the URL

After you upload your files, you have an Internet address! The URL for your address consists of the server name and a suffix. (Review the URL on the Prentice Hall server for the example web site we used in this section.) The "index.html" page has links to all the other pages in your site. After you FTP the page files, try out your URL. Pages should look just about as they did when you viewed them in the browser. If you wish to make changes at this point, change the pages on your computer using your web development software and upload them again.

An Alternate Strategy: Modifying Existing Pages

Another way of creating a web site is to "grab" an Internet page design you like and use it as a template for your own. Grabbing pages is easy. However, it is important to remember that many page elements (e.g., designs, logos, graphics) are copyrighted. Their legal use is determined by copyright law and by the owner of the web site. If you are not sure whether you can use page elements legally, contact the web site owner to request permission. In any event, always credit the source site on your page.

After you "grab" and save a page, be sure to place all the page elements in the same folder and re-insert the images and back-ground.

Try grabbing pages and modifying them in the following way:

- **Enter and copy the URL** – In your browser, enter the URL for the example web site (http://www.prenhall.com/startingout) and drag your mouse over the URL to copy it.

- **Open the page in *Netscape Composer*®** – Select **Open Page** from the **File Menu,** paste the URL, and open the page in *Netscape Composer*®.

- **Save the page** – Select **Save As** from the **File Menu.** (You may get a copyright warning at this point.) Save the page on your computer under a desired name.

- **Make desired changes** – Make changes as you like. Save the page and follow procedures for uploading it and its graphic elements to a server (Step 9).

Section Eleven
Summary Exercises: Creating Your Own Web Site

Exercises 11.1 – Review of New Terms and Concepts

_____ 1. The action of transferring new web pages to a server

_____ 2. Software required if you want to transfer page files from your computer to a server connected to the Internet

_____ 3. What you should make sure of before using a page element you have "grabbed" from an existing Internet site

_____ 4. Another name for a web page development software

_____ 5. An HTML command that indicates that an e-mail address follows and, when followed by your own e-mail address as a link from your web site, sends users who click on it to your e-mail address in their e-mail program

Exercises 11.2 – Practice Activities to Expand Your Skills

1. **Insert a rule** – Did you notice an extra graphic feature in the web page example? Bring up the Personal page and click below "G. L. Branch's Personal Page." Select **Horizontal Line** from the **Insert Menu**. Change its width by double-clicking on it and increasing its height.

2. **Add a background** – Add a background image instead of a background color. When you have a page in *Netscape Composer*®, select **Page Colors and Properties** from the **Format Menu**; click the **Colors and Background** tab and the **Use Image** box. Choose an image stored on your computer and click OK. What does it look like?

3. **Add and re-size a graphic** – Each of the free graphics sites has steps you must follow to obtain a graphic. Try one of them. Also try re-sizing the graphic. Double-click on it and change its height and width.

4. **Create your favorite links** – Most teachers list their own set of "favorite links" on their web site. Prepare your own set and insert them on your page as links to the sites.

5. **Preview in both browsers** – Sometimes pages look different in different browsers. Try previewing your page in *Internet Explorer*®. Does it look any different?

APPENDIX: Answers to Exercise Questions

Section One

Page 3
1. World Wide Web
2. kidlink
3. http://
4. "edu" shows it is owned by a higher education organization
5. slashes in "http://" are required to show it is an Internet address. Other slashes indicate suffixes.

Page 4
1. http://www.nctm.org
2. http://www.menc.org

Page 5 – top of page
1. American Federation for the Blind
2. U. S. Department of Education

Page 5 – bottom of page
1. Slashes are in the wrong direction
2. No dot between server name (ashaweb) and domain designator (org

Page 6: Exercises 1.1 – Review of New Terms and Concepts
1. domain designator
2. suffix
3. Uniform Resource Locator
4. spaces in server name
5. server

Page 6: Exercises 1.2 – Practice Activities to Expand Your Skills
1. http://www.aera.net
2. http://www.ira.org: International Reading Association
3. http://peabody.vanderbilt.edu: Peabody College of Education at Vanderbilt University
   a. "www" is omitted
   b. slashes are backward
   c. server name (Berkeley) is misspelled

Section Two

Page 10: Exercises 2.1 – Review of New Terms and Concepts

1. Both can be links
2. When you run the mouse over it, the pointer turns into a browser hand
3. The link has been clicked on previously
4. Look for a "Back to Home" link or use the Go Menu
5. It's a link

Page 10: Exercises 2.2 – Practice Activities to Expand Your Skills

Like many large sites, it has a pull-down menu of commonly-used links

Section Three

Page 15: Exercises 3.1 – Review of New Terms and Concepts

1. Subject index search
2. metacrawler
3. complete phrase
4. internal search engine
5. minus sign: "–"

Page 15: Exercises 3.2 – Practice Activities to Expand Your Skills, Set A

1. Enter "Trojan horse" –virus
2. "distance education" +journal +online
3. search on: writing +children +online
4. search on: "French to English" +dictionary

Page 15: Exercises 3.2 – Practice Activities to Expand Your Skills, Set B

1. keyword search using any search engine
2. Yahoo! subject index search; keyword search using any search engine
3. Yahoo! or Google subject index search
4. keyword search using any search engine
5. keyword search using any search engine
6. keyword search using any search engine
7. keyword search using any search engine
8. site internal search engine
9. Go to web sites recommended in this book and do site internal search
10. Go to web sites recommended in this book and do site internal search

Section Four

Page 20: Exercises 4.1 – Review of New Terms and Concepts

1. Favorites
2. Bookmarks Menu
3. File Menu
4. Folder
5. share them with others

Section Five

Page 26: Exercises 5.1 – Review of New Terms and Concepts

1. site map
2. internal search engine
3. known author, valid contact information, recent update, can be verified by authoritative sources
4. provides alternative ways to view information
5. navigation

Page 26: Exercises 5.2 – Practice Activities to Expand Your Skills

Sites have unknown authors, no valid contact information, have no indication of updates, and/or no sources or links to use to verify authenticate information

Section Six

Page 32: Exercises 6.1 – Review of New Terms and Concepts

1. firewall software
2. virus
3. firewall
4. parental involvement
5. filtering software

Page 32: Exercises 6.2 – Practice Activities to Expand Your Skills

3a. Contact the web site owner or administrator; if no contact information, use the element and credit the source
3b. Contact the web site owner or administrator for permission

Section Seven

Page 38: Exercises 7.1 – Review of New Terms and Concepts

1. gif
2. click on it
3. images on federal government web sites
4. copyright law and the owner of the web site
5. image manipulation software such as *Adobe PhotoShop*

Section Eight

Page 42: Exercises 8.1 – Review of New Terms and Concepts

1. pdf
2. plug-in
3. Quicktime®
4. portable document format
5. hear streamed audio files

Section Nine

Page 46: Exercises 9.1 – Review of New Terms and Concepts

1. bad or dead link (site has been removed or server is not working)
2. wait and try it again later; probably down temporarily
3. download the plug-in required to play it
4. your firewall software is preventing access
5. Javascript problem; make sure Java is enabled in browser or try downloading an updated Java version

Page 46: Exercises 9.2 – Practice Activities to Expand Your Skills

1. missing dot between "psu" and "edu"
2. missing colon (":") after http
3. apple spelled with a numeral one instead of a letter "l"
4. hyphens ("–") are used instead of underlines ("_")
5. zero in "com" instead of letter "o"

Section Ten

Page 52: Exercises 10.1 – Review of New Terms and Concepts

1. telementoring
2. electronic or virtual field trip
3. keypal or e-pal
4. social action projects
5. KidLink online activity and lesson plan site

Section Eleven

Page 70: Exercises 11.1 – Review of New Terms and Concepts

1. uploading
2. FTP software
3. you are permitted to use it
4. HTML editor
5. mailto